Jonty Allcock

The Christmas Thread

…nding *Joy* When Life Feels *Frayed*

Published by:
The Good Book Company

thegoodbook.com | thegoodbook.co.uk
thegoodbook.com.au | thegoodbook.co.nz

Every book published by The Good Book Company has been written by a human author and edited by a human editor. While AI tools are sometimes used to assist with research and support certain processes, all content has been created by a human author and thoroughly checked by our editorial team to ensure it is biblically faithful and pastorally wise.

Cover design by André Parker

ISBN: 9781802544510 | JOB-008602 | Printed in India

Imagine your life as a single
piece of thread...

Everyone has one.

Everyone has

ONLY ONE.

I wonder how you
feel about yours?

Most of us would instinctively say that this thread of life is...

PRECIOUS.

I didn't choose it.

I didn't earn it.

I didn't create it.

My life was a gift to me.

Every person has been given one life.
One thread. One chance.

We have equal dignity and worth.
Each thread is precious.
Something to be valued.
Something sacred.
Something to be lived to the full.

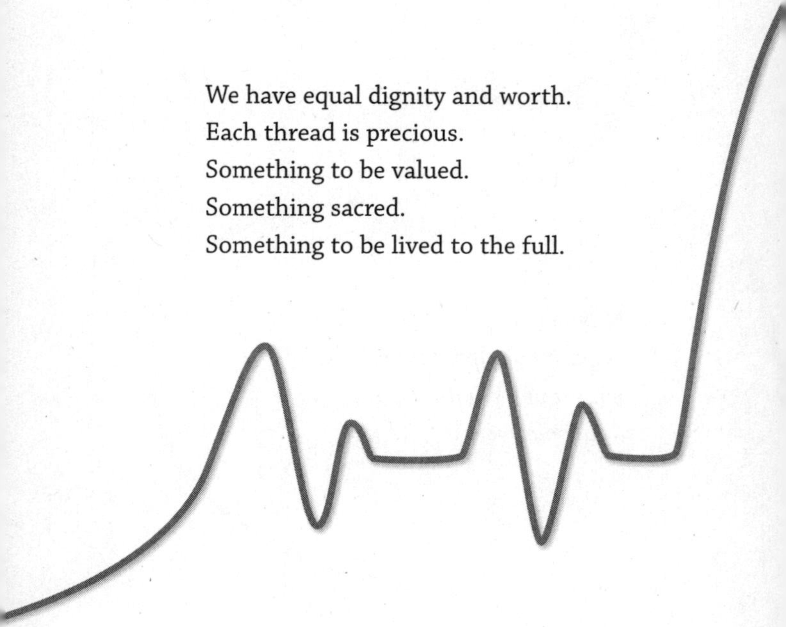

But isn't there also a part of you that finds this...

... a burden?

Maybe you find yourself thinking, *What if I waste it? What if I mess it up? What if my life is a disappointment?*

Suddenly we find that this precious gift begins to place a crushing weight of expectation on our shoulders. And so...

...we strive

and we try

and we attempt to
achieve great things so
that at the end of our
lives we can say,

***"I DID IT.
I MADE THE
MOST OF IT."***

I want to take my thread and stitch something that makes me feel proud so I can step back at the end of my life and say, "I am pleased with that".

I dream of weaving a masterpiece that deserves to be framed and hung on the wall of a gallery.

(To be honest, sewing has never really been my thing. My mum spent hours trying to guess what were the random creations I had brought home from school. "Well done darling, is it supposed to be a... fish?")

Of course there are some people who manage to take their lives and weave something spectacular. People like…

ALBERT EINSTEIN.

OR USAIN BOLT.

Or Taylor Swift.

By all human accounts,
Taylor Swift is doing
more than all right.

She's taken her thread
and maxed it out.

She's been TIME
Magazine's Person
of the Year. Twice.

She's broken 117
world records.

She has written
or co-written over
200 hit songs.

She has over 281
million followers
on Instagram.

She's worth an
estimated $2 billion.

Her cross-stitch is pretty impressive.

How about yours?

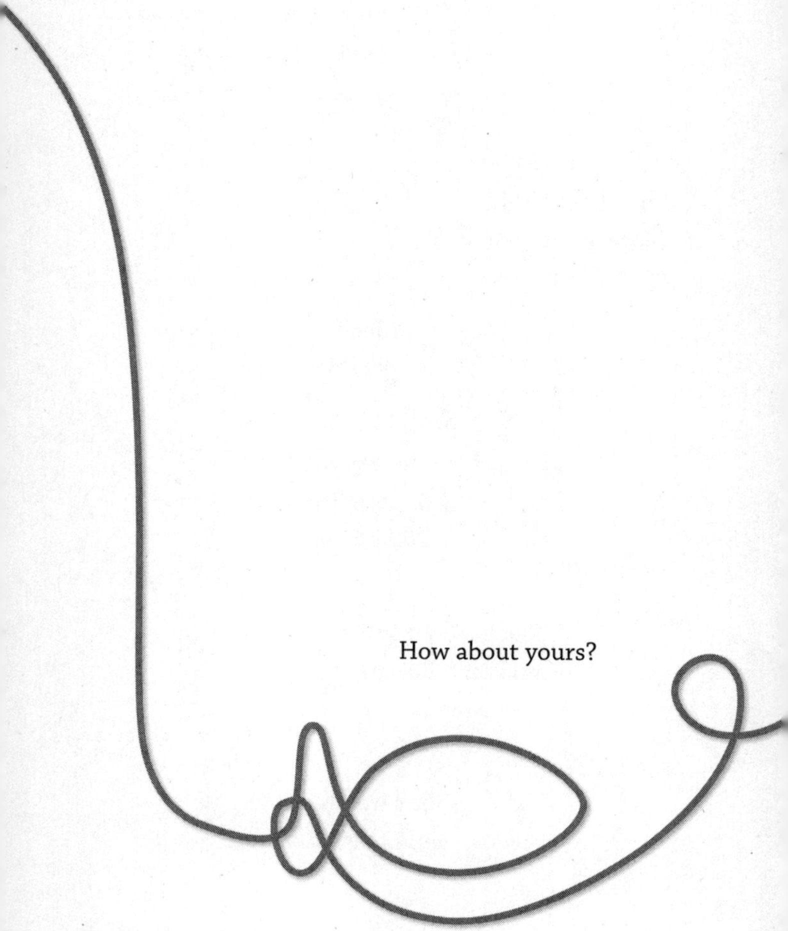

At Christmas, we often reflect on how our picture is looking.

Maybe it's because we catch up with friends and family we haven't seen for a while, and we can't help but compare our life with theirs. Or maybe this season reminds us that our thread is unravelling so quickly—we can't believe it's December again already.

What have we achieved with our single thread?

And sometimes it brings us face to face with the messes we've made—the knots in our picture that we can't untangle. People we've hurt. Patterns we're trapped in. Relationships we've lost. Risks we lack the courage to take.

But Christmas is good news for
people who feel ordinary.

And it's good news for people
who've got life tied up in knots...

because the real Christmas we
read about in the Bible—the story
of Jesus' birth 2,000 years ago—
begins with ordinary people.
It all starts with his mother,

Mary

She too had one life.
A single thread.

She was hardly setting the world on fire with her brilliance. She would not have had an enormous following on social media.

She was not a physically imposing athlete or ingenious academic.

She was just a teenager, probably about 15 years old, living in a small rustic village called Nazareth—a place most people had never heard of.

Her love interest was a carpenter called Joseph.

Even her name was deeply ordinary. At that time, in that culture, 20% of women were called Mary. So it wasn't even an interesting name.

Unlike Taylor Swift, Mary didn't write 200 songs—she only wrote one.

But here's the weird thing: 2,000 years later, people still sing Mary's song. They still ponder its meaning.

(However you feel about Taylor Swift, I am pretty confident people will not still be discussing her lyrics in a couple of millennia. What exactly did she mean by "Shake It Off"?).

And yet Mary's song—written by a nobody teenager in an ordinary place—has been recorded for us in the Bible and translated into over 2,000 languages. And countless millions of people have found, in the words of Mary's song, something so much deeper and more profound than anything in today's charts can offer.

So it's well worth taking that song and saying, *What did she mean?*

That first Christmas, Mary got a glimpse of a reality that set her soul on fire.

She saw something that made her heart sing.

Something that redefined her whole existence.

Mary was not being called to live an awesome individual life; she was being called to take her small place in a much bigger story.

It is not about what I can achieve with my one life and my single thread.

Rather, there is a God in heaven who is weaving a tapestry of intricate detail and mesmerising beauty. It is not made with one individual thread, but millions of threads woven together throughout human history, which tell one great story.

And when Mary understood that greater story, her heart burst forth in joy, and she wrote the best Christmas song of all.

If you'd like to experience a taste of that joy for yourself this Christmas, let me invite you to spend a few minutes looking at the lyrics.

"My soul glorifies the Lord
and my spirit rejoices in God my Saviour,
for he has been mindful
of the humble state of his servant.
From now on all generations will call me blessed,
for the Mighty One has done great things
for me—
holy is his name."

"His mercy extends to those who fear him,
        from generation to generation.
He has performed mighty deeds with his arm;
        he has scattered those who are proud in their
          inmost thoughts.
He has brought down rulers from their thrones
        but has lifted up the humble.
He has filled the hungry with good things
        but has sent the rich away empty.
He has helped his servant Israel,
        remembering to be merciful
to Abraham and his descendants for ever,
        just as he promised our ancestors."
(Luke 1:46-55)

Let's break that down a bit. First, she says...

"My soul glorifies the Lord and my spirit rejoices in God my Saviour."

Something has happened that has caused her a deep soul joy.
A joy that is lasting.
A joy that is solid.
Not the temporary joy of a bowl of ice cream that disappears once you've eaten it, but a joy that endures.

Mary has discovered this joy—not in herself. Not in her achievements. Not in her circumstances. But joy in God.

In the first half of this song, Mary says, *I'm singing for joy because of what God has done for me!*
So what is it that God has done?
Look how the song continues...

"For he has been mindful of the humble state of his servant. From now on all generations will call me blessed, for the Mighty One has done great things for me—holy is his name."

In other words, *My little thread has been caught up into God's greater story. God noticed me.*

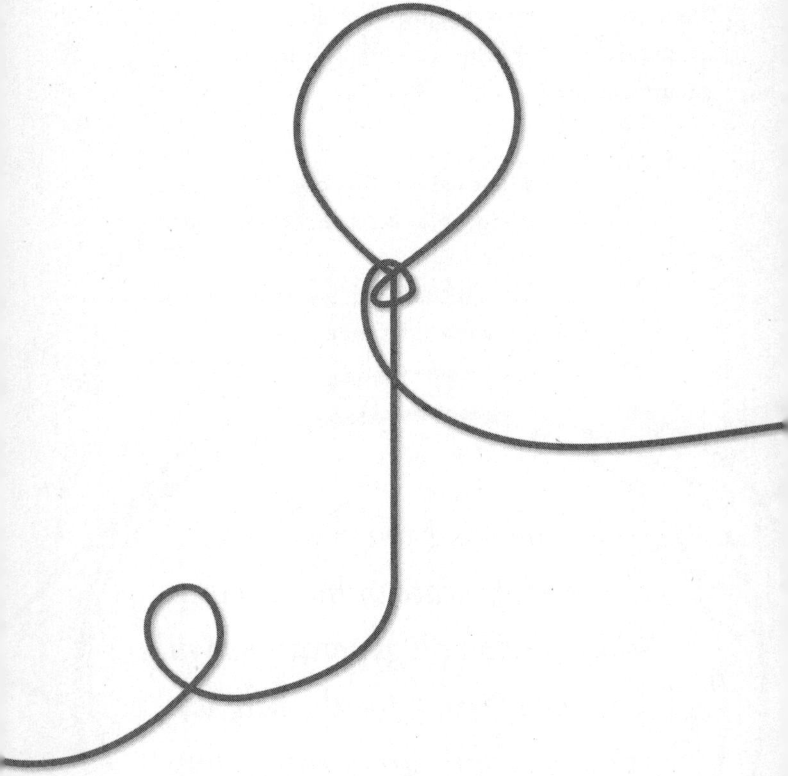

It's an extraordinary thing to be noticed, right?
To be noticed by someone who's significant.
To be noticed by someone who's important and who we care about.
And it's a horrible thing to be ignored.

We once hosted a birthday party for one of our kids.
A whole bunch of children came. We played some games and ate cake.
And at the end we sent them all home with party bags.
Except for one.

We just didn't see her.
We didn't notice.
I feel bad acknowledging it now. But this little girl, Izzy, didn't get a present.
She didn't say anything. She just went home. Sad.
The fact is, we hate to be ignored. And here is Mary saying...

The God of the universe has noticed me.

He's been mindful of me.

Okay, but why? Why has God noticed Mary?
Is it because she's so awesome?
Is it because she's great?
Is it because he's so impressed by her?

No.

She says he's been "mindful" of her "humble state".
He noticed me even though I'm not all that.
This is the great message of Christmas.
The God that we read of in the Bible—the God who created everything—notices the humble.
We don't have to shine the brightest or shout the loudest in order to impress him.
He sees us as we are.

But God doesn't just see Mary.
Look what she says next...
"From now on all generations will call me blessed".
God notices her, and he blesses her.

BLESS.

That's a big word, right?

It means to do good things for someone.
It is a really important word in the Bible.
Right back near the start, God appeared to a man named Abraham and said, "I will bless you".
Abraham was nobody special, just like Mary.
He lived in a city called Ur.

Can you imagine a more unimpressive-sounding place?
"What should we call this place?"

"Err…."

"Great! That'll do."
Abraham wasn't famous. He wasn't doing anything significant. And yet God said…
"I will bless you".

Through this man Abraham, and
through his family, a great story began
to be woven in which God says,

I will bless you,
I will pour out my love on you.
I will protect you.
You will be mine.
You will be my treasured possession.

From that beginning, the picture grew as God wove together the threads of many generations that followed on from Abraham: characters in the Bible like...

Ruth—a foreign widow who found her place in a strange land.

Joseph—the slave who God used to save the world.

And David—the shepherd boy who became a king.

Many ordinary, individual lives. Woven together.
Hundreds, thousands, millions of threads.
All the way down to Mary.
Don't miss how extraordinary this is.

If you feel that you are a nobody,
if you feel that no one is really
interested in you,
if you feel that your life is dull,
if you feel that you're unimpressive,
here is the great news...

God notices people like...

YOU.

He sees you—and he sees you in order that he might bless you.
That's his great purpose: that he might welcome you into his family.
That you might become his child.
That you might know his love.
That he might say...

This one is mine.

And God doesn't stop there...

... because in the next line of her song, Mary says... "The Mighty One has done great things for me—holy is his name".

This is remarkable maturity for a teenager. Especially when you consider that, in the story so far, the main thing Mary has experienced is an angel telling her that she's going to have a baby.

And not just any baby: a baby who's going to be God's Son and the King for ever.

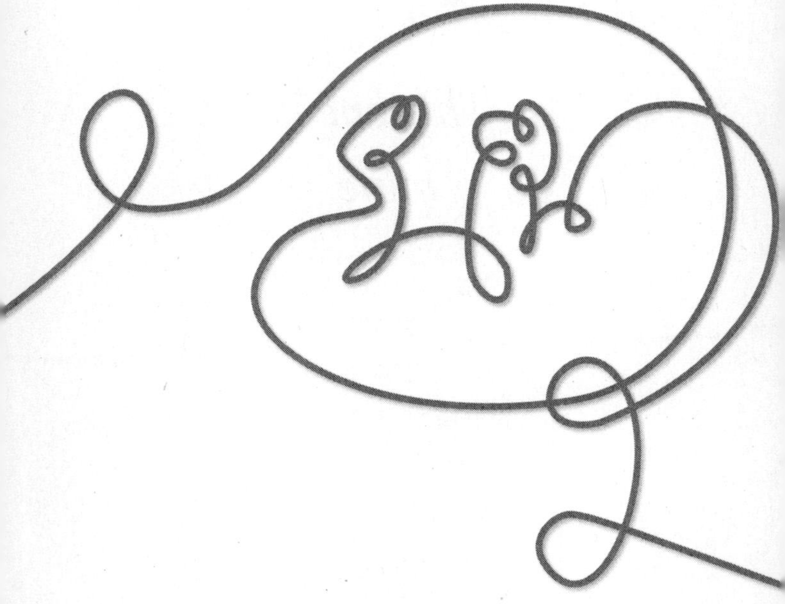

But rather than freak out, Mary says,
It's a great thing he's done for me...
because Mary knew that the baby who would be born—the baby that she carried in her womb—was the King.
The King who would come to save Mary and to save all those who will trust him.
Mary is part of this story. So she sings...

He noticed me.
He blessed me.
He's done great things for me.
From me will come a king!

But then her song makes a switch in the second verse.
She moves on from talking about "me" and "my".
Now she says, *That's what God is always like.*
"His mercy extends to those who fear him,
from generation to generation."

This is what God has always done.
What God did for Mary is what God has always done through history, to all those who will "fear him".

That doesn't mean we need to be terrified of him. It means to say...

You are God,
you are **great**,
and I am
small.

His kindness and forgiveness are for all who will admit that they need him.
God notices.
God blesses.
God does great things.

But there's a warning here...

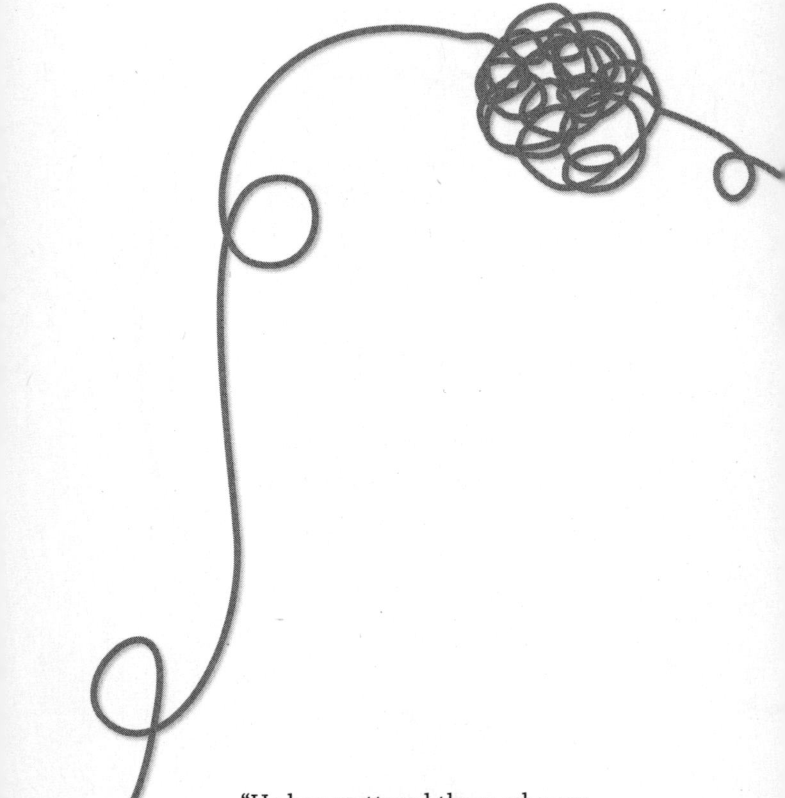

… "He has scattered those who are
proud in their inmost thoughts. He has
brought down rulers from their thrones
but has lifted up the humble."

You see, those who want to be impressive on their own, those who want to say,
"No, no, no, this is my life".
"I will create my picture myself—and I will create something awesome."

Those who want to lift themselves up like that,

God will bring down.

This is how God always operates.
It's so different to the way we think.
In our world, everybody wants to go up.
That's the game, right? We're all trying to climb up.
We teach kids that. We learn it early in school.

We sing about a spider who
climbs up the water spout...
Because up is good.

"Down came the rain and washed the spider out."
Oh no, the poor little spider has gone down!
Never mind children, he'll have another go.

Come on, boys and girls, let's keep climbing!
It's the same with that most famous of boardgames. You go up the ladders and then—oh no!—you're sliding down again. But it's all heading up. Everything's up.

But God says the way to be blessed is to go down, not up.

To say, *It's not about me.*
It's not about how impressive I am because, honestly, I'm not that impressive.

I get things wrong all the time. I'm the problem. It's me.

(Which is also a lyric from the Taylor Swift song "Anti-Hero". Even she knows it.)

And actually, that's the tension in every
human heart.
That even as I try to go up,
even as I try to create this amazing life,
even as I try to achieve everything and try
to show the world how great I am...
there's something in me that says...
But I'm the problem.

I feel insecure.
I feel like an impostor.
I feel like a fraud all the time.
I make a mess.
I'm the problem.
And that's true.
The cross-stitch of our lives might look fine
from the front—impressive, even.
But flip it over...

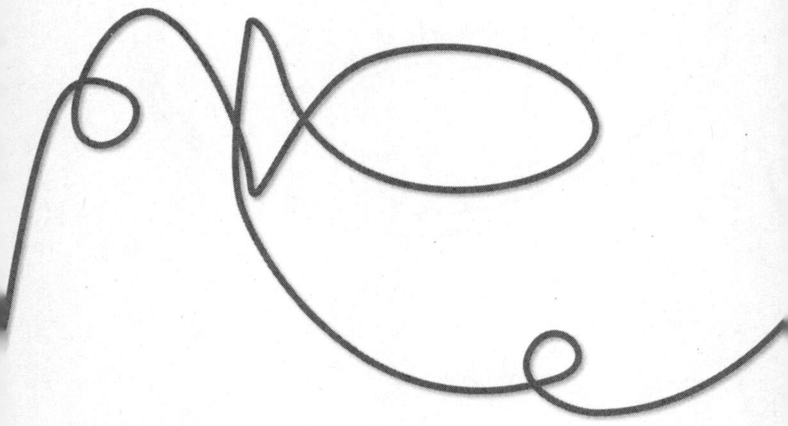

... and you soon find a mess.
We do have a problem, and the problem is us.
The problem is that we are proud and want to achieve things for ourselves.
We want to make a name for ourselves.
And we don't care all that much about who we have to ignore or push aside in the process. Not really.
The problem is that we want to be great—we want to be the god of our own lives, stitching our own picture on our own terms.
But God says that is not the way to be blessed.

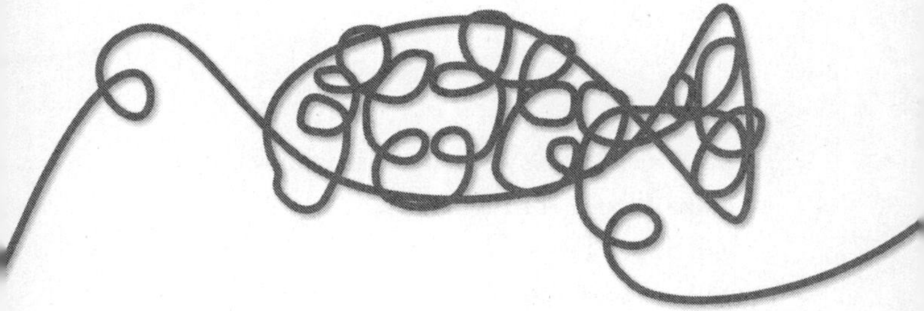

Mary's song tells us that those who want to
make a name for themselves
will be scattered,
will be shattered,
will be brought down.
But those who know they're the problem,
those who are humble,
those who come saying, "Please help me, God..."
to those God says...

"I will lift you up".
Mary expressed something similar in the very next line: "He has filled the hungry with good things but has sent the rich away empty".
If you come to God saying, "I don't need anything from you. I've got everything I need. I'm sorted. My life is awesome..." then he has nothing for you. God will send you away empty.

But if you come to God, saying...
"I'm in trouble. I've made a mess of my life. My thread is in knots. I've done things wrong—things I feel ashamed of"...

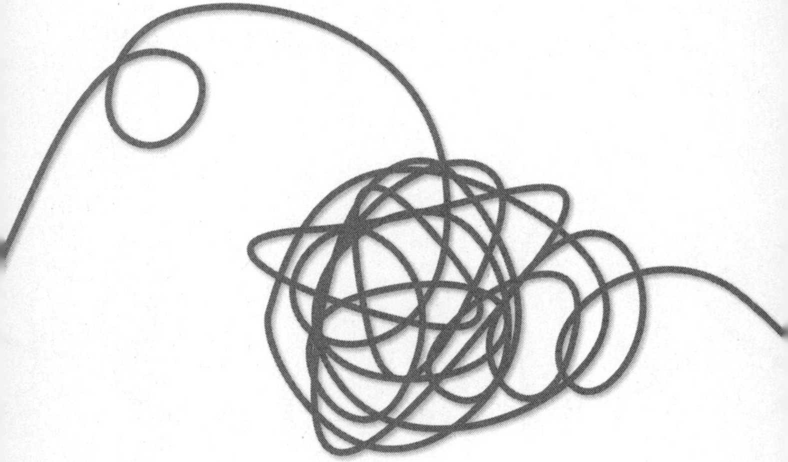

To you he says, *Come to me. I will help you.*
This is how God works.
He does not reward the high achievers.
He rescues those who are lowly.
He forgives those who admit they've got it wrong.
He blesses those who know they need him.
This is what he does, and it is exactly how Jesus lived his life.

Even though he was King over all things,
every day of his life, Jesus chose

to stoop down,
not reach up.

Every day of his
life, Jesus chose to
empty himself, not
to fill himself.

Every day of his life, Jesus chose to serve people, not to be served himself.
Every day of his life, Jesus chose down—until eventually, at the age of 33, he was nailed to a cross.
He went to the very lowest place and died.

And the reason that Jesus died was so that
you could be lifted up.
This is what God does.

He lifts up the humble.

He feeds the hungry.

He loves the unlovely.

He has mercy on the wrongdoers.

He forgives all those who ask.
It's beautiful.

So Mary finishes by singing...

"He has helped his servant Israel, remembering to be merciful to Abraham and his descendants for ever, just as he promised our ancestors."

She says, *This is my story—the story that starts all the way back with Abraham.*

Mary is now part of that story. And here's the really great thing.

YOU COULD BE TOO.

You could be part of that story because the story still continues.
Because Jesus, the baby who was born in Bethlehem and who grew up to die on the cross... he rose to life again.
He lives today. He is King of kings.
Now, the story is not confined to one nation or ethnicity.

Now, to all who will come to him, he says, *I'll notice you, and I will forgive you, and I will bless you, and I will do great things for you.*
He untangles our knotted-up thread, and he weaves it into something beautiful.
Something that gives us solid joy like Mary's—now and for ever.
That's what he does for all who come to him with empty hands.

But to the proud,
to the arrogant,
to those who say,
"No, I'll sort my own life out, thanks..."
those people he sends away empty.
And that's a serious thing,
because no matter how good a picture we manage to stitch for ourselves, all of us run out of thread eventually.
Life ends.
And then what?

Christmas shows us that there is a choice to make.
Do we come to this King, humble and empty, and say,
"Please forgive me and fill me"?
Or do we reject him and say, "I don't want you—I'll do things myself"?
In these last few pages, I want to show you what it looks like to say to Jesus,
"Please forgive me and fill me".
We've heard an ancient song from the Bible.
But God still works in peoples' lives today.
So here's the story of how another ordinary person's knotted-up thread was woven into something beautiful when he came to God with empty hands.

Harry's story

I didn't grow up knowing about Jesus. I was just trying to work out what life was all about. I often found myself pretending to be someone that wasn't really me.

I wanted to be successful. I wanted to be impressive. I wanted people to approve. But I also wanted to be my own person and not care about what others thought of me. It was a confusing mix and left me feeling insecure. *Do people really know me? Or do they only know the "me" that I let them see?* I found myself regularly gripped by loneliness and shame, my mental health took a real hit, and I became addicted to things that led me deeper into shame.

Then two things happened that began a process of change. Firstly, I started reading a book by C.S. Lewis. To be honest, my initial motivation was just to appear more intellectual. But the book stirred something very different in me. For the first time I read about the God who had created all things. I read of his beauty and love, and it was amazing. I was compelled.

But it also made me look more honestly at the real me rather than the person I pretended to be. I saw that my heart was a mess. It was hard to hide the truth from the God who had made me.

The second thing that happened was that a friend invited me to go to church. I don't know why, but I found I wanted to go. I felt self-conscious and uncomfortable as I took my seat. It was so weird and unfamiliar. I was a spectator watching something I had never seen before. It was particularly the singing that was so striking. People seemed to mean it. They seemed full of joy.

The more I went, the more I understood of God's love for the world. I decided to give it a go and pretend to be a Christian. I prayed. I read the Bible. I even tried the singing. But it still seemed to be fake. I kept it external and didn't allow it to touch my heart. I was still struggling with addiction and didn't find the hope that I knew I desperately needed.

Then one day, I was listening to a talk that explained again why Jesus had to die. Suddenly it all clicked into place. God came to forgive me. Jesus died for my sin. I didn't have to pretend because God knew the truth about me already. It was so simple. I asked God to forgive me. I asked him to set me free.

I tasted the joy that Mary felt. The joy of knowing that God was mindful of me. The joy of knowing that I could be part of the bigger story.

Harry, living in London

Everything Mary sang about, God is still doing in the world: noticing, blessing, doing great things, taking the lowly and lifting them up this Christmas. That could be you.

If you'd like that to be your story this Christmas, you could start by praying this prayer:

Heavenly Father, thank you for Christmas.
Thank you so much that being known and loved by God is not about how hard I work or how much I achieve.
Thank you for what you have done on the cross.
Thank you for your great story.
Father, I pray that this Christmas I would find my part in your great story.
I come to you with empty hands. Please fill me.
I know that I'm the problem. Please forgive me.
Thank you that Jesus was brought low so that I can be lifted up.
Please help me to know the freedom and joy he brings.
In Jesus' name, amen.

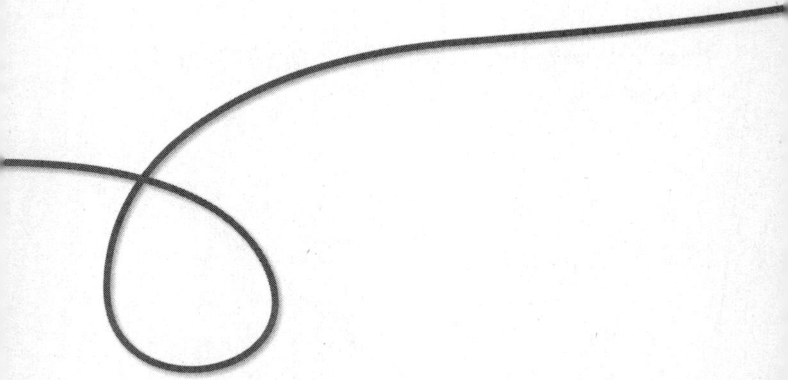

About the author

Jonty Allcock is pastor at The Globe Church in central London. He is married to Linda and loves being a dad to three sons. Jonty is the author of several books, including *Happily Ever After* and *More of Jesus*.

thegoodbook COMPANY

Thanks for reading this book. We hope you enjoyed it and found it helpful.

Most people want to find answers to the big questions of life: Who are we? Why are we here? How should we live? But we are often unable to find the time or space to think positively and carefully about them.

At The Good Book Company, we're passionate about producing resources that help people of all ages and stages to understand the heart of the Christian message, found in the pages of the Bible, and to see how that message provides answers to our biggest questions.

So whoever you are and wherever you are at, we hope we can help you to think things through. Visit our website to discover the range of books and other resources we publish, both for people who are looking into Christianity and those who have already made the decision to follow Jesus. Or head to our partner site at christianityexplored.org/what-is-christianity for a clear explanation of who Jesus is and why he came.

Thanks again for reading.

Your friends at The Good Book Company